REMOTE ABILITY

REMOTE ABILITY

12 Tactics to Manage the Culture
of Your Suddenly Remote Team

RUSS HILL, JARED JONES, & TANNER CORBRIDGE

Remote Ability: 12 Tactics to Manage the Culture of Your Suddenly Remote Team

ISBN: 978-1-7363374-0-0

First Edition

Interior design: Adina Cucicov

TABLE OF CONTENTS

INTRODUCTION

Russ was walking out of a meeting in the Washington DC area when a senior executive stopped him and asked, "Why don't we do the next meeting virtually?"

> *(This book has three co-authors: Russ Hill, Jared Jones, and Tanner Corbridge. That's why you'll read the word "we" a lot in this book. We'll share more about our background in the coming pages, but we should probably get back to Russ's story. He gets mad when we interrupt his stories. That's sarcasm by the way—expect more.)*

Russ had just finished facilitating two days of intense discussions among some of the leaders of a Fortune 100 company. The executives were deep in the work of trying to shift their culture to accelerate the results they needed to deliver. Our conversations those two days had been emotional but productive. Most participants had flown in for the meeting at the company's headquarters.

"These meetings don't work virtually. Sorry. We know that would be a lot easier, but we'll need to get everyone back here in person as soon as possible," Russ said, as he wheeled his luggage out of the room and raced off to the airport.

Then, Covid happened.

Guess what Russ discovered? He was wrong. Embarrassingly wrong. (Happens a lot, actually.) Okay, maybe we all held the same belief. You probably did too. Most of us thought things we did in person wouldn't translate to the virtual world.

Russ and some of our colleagues met again with those executives who were in the meeting near DC more than half a dozen times in the following months. All of those meetings have been virtual. All have been remarkably productive. That company's culture is moving in the right direction. It turns out that culture can be managed effectively remotely! We have witnessed it over and over again with the diverse set of companies we're privileged to work with.

WHY THIS BOOK?

If you're looking for a book on how to use Zoom, Teams, or WebEx, this ain't that. Sure, we can show you how to unmute yourself before speaking brilliance that no one heard, but our real expertise is in culture management. We—the three co-authors of this book—have nearly four decades of consulting experience with leaders like you on how to manage culture and create accountability for results.

Remoteability isn't just about how to conduct virtual meetings and how to interact with remote teams. It's also about how we engage our people and our customers in a completely different way. Any leader who isn't consciously adjusting their leadership style to this brand-new world is failing to demonstrate remoteability.

Some of you may be reading this thinking the new work environment is temporary. Perhaps you're expecting that in just a few months, everything will be back to normal and everyone will return to their desk in an office building again. You probably thought Covid-19 would be a three-month interruption too, though! Betting against change or disruption is a quick way to lose money.

While none of us can predict the future with certainty, we're pretty confident that work life will never look exactly like it did pre-Covid. This work-from-home genie isn't going back in the bottle. A 2020 Global Workplace Analytics Survey found that 76 percent of people said that they want to continue working remotely after the pandemic ends. If we had to guess, based on our interaction with leaders in many companies, we'd predict that a hybrid approach is the future. That hybrid will feature a lot less business travel, a mixture of in-person and virtual meetings, and a schedule comprised of at-home and in-office work weeks. That new environment demands that we all lead differently. Buckle up: We've all got a lot of adjustments to make to how we lead our teams!

THE 10-80-10 PRINCIPLE

We live in a time of constant disruption. (For instance, Jared is a diehard Patriots fan. We like to remind him a lot about the disruption he's been going through.) On a much more serious note, Covid-19 is arguably the biggest disruption in decades. But it's not the only one and it won't be the last. Massive and constant changes in customer and employee expectations are also driving significant disruption.

When disruptions occur, people tend to segment into three groups. It's called the 10-80-10 Principle.

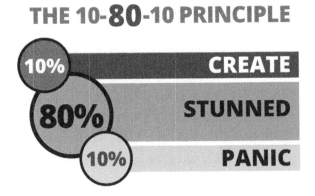

The principle states that when disruption happens, **10 percent of people go into Panic Mode.** This group responds to disruption in one of two ways. They crawl into the fetal position in the corner sucking on a bottle of status quo, hoping their tenure will convince the destroying angel to pass over them. Or they douse their noggin with hair spray, light a match, and scream all kinds of impractical ideas as they run through the house at full speed, hoping their urgency will cause others to think they've "got this." (Someone, please grab the fire extinguisher!)

Another group is made up of **the 80 percent of people who slide into Stunned Mode.** These folks did not expect the disruption and aren't sure what to do in response to it. People in this group aren't paralyzed or crazy but rather are sitting on their hands waiting for someone to tell them what to do. This is the group waiting for the cavalry to come over the distant hilltop and save them, when we actually need them to "saddle up!" They justify their lack of movement with their willingness to innovate or do things differently. They say they're willing to be agile but actually aren't. Part of them doesn't want to commit to trying a "new way" in case it turns out that hard work wasn't really needed. Think of the fad diet crowd, not treadmill warriors. They're head nodders, rather than early adopters. These folks often have great intentions but a ton of muscle memory.

The third group is the roughly **10 percent of people who jump immediately into Create Mode** when disruption strikes.

These are the innovators. They are the ones who have been vocal proponents of change for years. They knew the future demanded a new way of doing things and hoped someone would eventually listen to them. The people in this group are totally comfortable driving in fog. Their minds are thinking, "Why pull over and wait when you can slow down a little, turn on the headlights, and keep moving?" The destination is so ingrained in their minds that they literally have never even thought about visiting a rest stop. While the panicked group is freaking out, this group can't believe a moment of opportunity this big has finally arrived.

Keep in mind that where people sit on an org chart has nothing to do with which group they fall into when disruptions hit. We've seen senior executives in Panic Mode and plenty of individual contributors in Create Mode.

The 10-80-10 Principle generates a couple of questions for you:

QUESTION ONE: Which group are you in? *(Are you sure?)*

QUESTION TWO: How do you get more people on your team into Create Mode?

Self-awareness is critical when how we work is changing so dramatically. If you're in Panic Mode, get help fast! Let go of whatever got you to this point in your career because there's no way that it will unlock opportunity in the future or help your team deliver results now. In other words, Panic Mode = Career Killer.

If you're in Stunned Mode, stop waiting for direction! There are two groups that can help you deliver results and bring value immediately: customers and colleagues in Create Mode. Get as close to both as you can and ask tons of questions. Listen to what the customer needs and wants and consider the ideas being proposed by the innovators around you. Where possible, give more visibility and responsibility to those in Create Mode and reassign or part ways with those who are stuck in Panic Mode.

To those of you in Create Mode, keep offering ideas! You must realize that only 10 percent of the team or organization is as comfortable as you are in the current environment. Keep talking with customers and speaking up and sharing what you're hearing. Don't wait for permission to try new things—in appropriate ways, of course—and don't slow down! The more you evangelize innovation and how it can immediately impact results, the greater support you'll likely find.

One word of caution for you innovators: Some of your organizations won't survive. As you offer ideas with urgency and patience, some of you will discover that your team, division, or company are led by people who are completely stuck in Panic or Stunned Mode. When and where appropriate, you may have to consider changing where you work. We coach more than a few leaders who have discovered in recent months that their company or boss are in total Panic Mode. Those have been some very tough calls, as we've heard leaders we've built strong relationships with over the years stare at choices that aren't easy.

STORIES OF CHANGE

We feel like we're three of the luckiest people alive. We consult for some incredible companies. You'd recognize the names and brands of many of them. They're well-known restaurant chains, manufacturers, healthcare companies, defense contractors, insurance brands, retailers, and energy companies. Due to non-disclosure agreements, and because lawyers can sound scary, you won't read most of their names on these pages. But you will hear their stories! Stories about how they're navigating the massive shift to leading remotely. We've spent most of the last year logged into virtual meeting rooms with them as they've dealt with massive shifts in customer demand, supply chain disruptions, resource reduction, reduced travel, employee fatigue, mute buttons, and offices they're now sharing with dogs and kids.

The demands on leaders have never been heavier. A huge amount of uncertainty and unending changes in every aspect of our lives don't relieve us of the expectation to deliver results. But, where's the new leadership playbook? Are there best practices that can help us hit our targets in this newly dispersed work environment?

That's why we wrote this book. We are confident that it will prove to be *a practical, timely guide you can quickly consume and immediately implement.* The ideas we share here are all designed to do one thing: help you deliver results. We don't advocate focusing on culture because it makes work more fun or enjoyable. Those things are nice byproducts of culture, but they aren't THE reason to work on culture. We work on culture because your team or organization's culture is producing your results.

Managing culture is a skillset that has proven to be a game changer over and over again. The companies we advise hire us to help them shift their culture. Organizations have cultures but so do teams. Your team has a culture. That culture is producing results. If you need different results, then you need shifts in your culture. We wrote this book to help you manage your team's culture—and do it entirely or partially remotely.

Culture is the way people think and act to get things done. When we use the word *culture* in this book, we're not talking about ping pong tables and new perks designed to make people happy. Culture can persuade a 16-year-old high school student in a drive-through to make you believe that she is thrilled you came to order a chicken sandwich and actually cares what your name is! Culture can produce a system that allows you to click a button on your phone and somehow trigger the movement of an item from a gigantic warehouse to your front porch overnight or in a few hours. Culture triggers a decision by a pilot to push a wheelchair down a jetbridge rather than leave it to someone else to do.

Managing culture isn't a soft skill. It has the potential to be your—we're talking directly to you right now—competitive advantage. Don't be fooled by the thickness of this book. We say this with tons of humility, but what you're holding right now has the potential to be a game changer for you as a leader. How do we know? Because of what we've seen happen when leaders start to intentionally manage their culture. This book will get you started on that path. And it will show you how to do it remotely!

NOW TO THE 12 TACTICS...

So, with that huge expectation raiser (maybe we should have underpromised and overdelivered—hmmmm), we want to walk you through how we structured the pages ahead. We broke this up into 12 tactics. The 12 tactics are things you can do immediately to begin managing the culture of your team. How did we pick these 12? We actually started with five based on observations we made in the first few months of most teams beginning to work at home. We worked with some teams that seemed to be stuck in the Stunned or Panic Mode (some are still there), while others quickly transitioned into the Create Mode. Everyone's game plan was thrown out the window. Some adapted and shifted quickly while others are struggling to get movement and traction.

After presenting what we called "the 5 Leadership Competencies During Uncertainty" in a live webinar that more than

3,000 people participated in, we started helping some of our clients implement them. That exposed additional skills and competencies that were clearly critical to helping remote teams deliver results. Ultimately, our list grew to 12 tactics that we're now ready to share with leaders around the globe.

These are the 12 tactics we see leaders demonstrate that create a culture of delivering results on remote teams:

We wrote this book to be more like a series of YouTube videos than a dissertation. It's designed to be consumed quickly and easily. We wanted you to be able to read a tactic (chapter) between virtual meetings or while waiting to pick up a child from soccer practice. Most of us have less alone time than we used to, with few or no commutes to the office or long flights to meetings or vacation spots. This book is designed to fit into your current schedule.

ACCESS THE ONLINE TRAINING

Check out the free virtual training on these topics by accessing the website that accompanies this book.

Access the free online training videos by going to **www.remoteabilitybook.com.**

CREATE CLARITY

----

12 TACTICS

1. **CREATE CLARITY**
2. GENERATE ALIGNMENT
3. BUILD ACCOUNTABILITY
4. BE VISIBLE
5. BE ACCESSIBLE
6. BE TRANSPARENT
7. INCREASE AGILITY
8. DEMONSTRATE EMPATHY
9. MANAGE BELIEFS
10. RUN EFFECTIVE MEETINGS
11. VALIDATE AUTHENTICITY
12. ENSURE WELL-BEING

As February 2020 came to a close, Russ looked at his calendar wondered how he was going to survive March. "You guys are not going to see much of me at all next month," he warned his wife and kids. Russ had flights booked to 10 different cities across the U.S. and Europe. Some involved new clients that had just signed substantial agreements. Then he started seeing news stories about a virus sweeping across China.

"This woman wearing a mask actually just wiped down the entire chair next to me," he said into his AirPods on a call to his wife. Russ was waiting to board a flight in the DFW Airport. "You wouldn't believe how paranoid this lady is," he said in a mocking voice he'd later regret when he began the habit of bathing in hand sanitizer a few times a day.

That flight home was the last plane Russ got on for five months. We all—and likely you, too, if you were a frequent traveler—never expected to spend so many consecutive nights in our own bed. None of us will ever forget March 2020.

In a matter of moments, our calendars became complete messes. Flights cancelled. Meetings postponed. People sent home. A new thing called Zoom Invites. Emergency meetings. Offices shuttered. An immediate round of furloughs. Then another one. Dining rooms closed. Curbside pickup became a thing. Empty shelves at the stores. New terms like PPP and PPE. Kids needing computers and help logging into class. And our homes needing faster Wi-Fi—now!

In a moment, our lives changed in dramatic and unexpected ways because of a virus. No one saw it coming or had any clue it could spread across the globe so fast. As leaders, we were suddenly operating in the thickest of fogs. Visibility was reduced to a day or two. We were left unable to answer questions about next month or even next week. How scary was that?

 Uncertainty leads to confusion. Confusion destroys speed and efficiency.

As we write these words, much of the fog has lifted, but it's not completely gone. Visibility into the future has increased, but none of us can speak with much confidence about anything further than three to six months down the road.

THE NEW WORK ENVIRONMENT

It used to be that when you wondered what people were working on or what the mood of the team was, you could just walk the floor and find out. You'd lean over to a member of your team before a meeting and do a quick check-in. You'd stop by someone's cubicle and clarify the meaning of an email from earlier in the day. "They couldn't possibly have meant to come across the way they sounded," you thought. Or you'd watch body language as people filed into conference rooms or came back from lunch.

But in the suddenly virtual work world, those moments of interaction and checking in look totally different. How do you detect the mood of your team? How do you ensure people are working on the right things and prioritizing tasks in a way that helps achieve the results you need to deliver? Add to that the challenge of making sure your team is doing an effective job managing all the distractions that come from working at home.

That's why creating clarity has to be Tactic One!

Your team needs clarity around the results you need them to deliver and clarity around your expectations of what they're doing each day to deliver those results. This is where account-ability begins: clearly defined outcomes. We'll define and talk more in a moment about two critical terms to Remoteability: Key Results and Key Expectations.

Before we do, we have to share an experience that blew our minds. We're old enough to remember working in office buildings. You've seen them, right? Those are the wide or tall buildings with empty parking lots and big banners hanging on them that say, "Space available." It was during that era that a senior executive we'll call Sally excitedly asked us to follow her into a conference room. One of the long walls alongside the conference room table was a floor-to-ceiling white board. The board had been attacked by a whole variety of colored markers and was covered with words, phrases, and drawings. Visualize a cave wall covered in drawings with an archaeologist standing ready to inter-pret the cryptic visual.

Sally bragged to us about how many fabulous ideas her team had captured on the board during their recent full-day brain-storming session. As she smiled and pointed at the wall, we struggled to hide what we were thinking and feeling. It was like the room was spinning. Our eyes begged for help finding a place to focus on. Almost out of desperation we asked, "Which of the ideas did you decide to pursue?"

Make sure you're sitting down right now. If you're listening to the audio version of this book, consider stepping away from the lawn mower or off the treadmill for a moment. Sally responded to our question and said, "All of them!" Oh, the horror! Don't say we didn't warn you this was going to get ugly.

All of them? Yes, she said. Her team left the meeting planning to focus on all of the ideas on the wall. As tragic as this story sounds, it's happening everywhere. KPI might be the worst three letters ever stacked together. How can 150 things be "KEY" Performance Indicators? Jumbotrons everywhere claim no relation to things called "balanced scorecards." Remind us how many figures on a scorecard fans and players really care about during a game.

 Here's the punchline: The leader who is trying to deliver it all rarely delivers what matters most.

We pay leaders to make decisions. To narrow the team's focus. It's hard to reach a destination if the leader wants to drive down every side street. Highways have crowded onramps for a reason. We want to get where we're trying to go—FASTER! Guess what? Leaders drive the team's bus. And far too many leaders are swerving far too much—focused mostly on avoiding the obstacles in the road and not crashing into a ravine. Your team needs clarity and focus. And in this remote environment, they need it more than ever!

ACTIVITY VERSUS RESULTS

We're going to take you behind the curtain in a moment and show you what we're seeing in many of the companies you admire for their extraordinary success. We'll show you HOW leaders of those companies are getting their teams focused on what matters most, but first we have to make one more point that is so critical to understand.

Part of the problem getting a team to deliver results is that they actually think they're crushing it. We should pose a question rather than give away the answer too quickly here. What do you think most employees measure success by? In other words, what metric do they use to determine whether they're a valuable employee of this company today? The metric is often this thing called ACTIVITY. Yes, that's a problem. Guess what exactly none of us get paid to do: stay busy with transactional activity! And yet, the vast majority of employees are gauging their contribution by how busy they are or how much activity they're generating.

Please introduce us to the shareholder that values activity! Show us the board member that hands out trophies for being super busy. One of the most significant shifts a leader can help their team make is understanding they're paid to deliver results. You might wonder how in the world all these people on all these teams across so many companies got screwed up thinking they were paid to stay busy doing stuff. The answer is their leaders! Guess what your team hears you talk about the most? Activity! The STUFF everyone is doing. Meetings, one-on-ones, and huddles rarely focus on results. "That's not true," you're screaming at this page. "We talk about results all the time in our meetings and one-on-ones," you say. Okay, let's have this conversation. Which results are you talking about in those meetings? "All of them," you say. Okay. Thanks, Sally! (Remember the white board with all the writing on it! Yup— many of us are Sally, and we don't even know it!)

THE NURSING HUDDLE

To illustrate our point, we want to take you inside a hospital pre-Covid. We work with a good number of hospital systems. In one visit to a hospital in Virginia, Jared was invited by a nursing supervisor to attend the 7am huddle that happens every morning at shift change. The overnight team briefs the daytime crew about anything significant. These nurses work in the Oncology Unit where patients are typically fighting serious disease. Jared listened as the nurses exchanged information on patients and then watched as their leader finished the huddle pointing to a bulletin board. She said, "I want to do a quick update on our results." She pointed to one sheet of paper stapled to the board. Then another. Then another. Jared started feeling dizzy. Another leader pointing to a wall covered in priorities.

The metrics that hospital is measuring are important. We're not recommending ignoring all metrics at the expense of a few. We are suggesting that the best leaders we work with take the complex and make it simple. They value focus and alignment above complexity and busy work. It's likely that all the metrics you're working on matter in some way. And yet, we're obligated to tell you what differentiates the teams we work with that achieve extraordinary results and those that are busy but not moving the needle. One of the biggest differences is a leader who clarifies what matters most and then maintains a discipline to drive down the middle of the road toward that destination.

CLARIFY YOUR KEY RESULTS

We're overdue for quoting some statistics in this book. The Partners In Leadership 2020 Culture Advantage Index revealed 84% of employees believe their organizational results are not clearly defined. It's hard to hold people accountable for delivering results when more than 8 out of 10 of them aren't clear on what they are.

When we say "Key Results," we're talking about three metrics that by themselves define success for the next year. We say three because that's what the science shows people can remember without any assistance (aka the Trinity Theory).

Each Key Result should include a one simple category and one simple metric (like Revenue: $30 million; Patient Experience: Top Quartile; or Quality: 10% Defect Reduction). Key Results don't describe things like "collaborate more" or "communicate effectively." Those are ways we may need to work better together as a team, but they don't define what needs to happen. We'll dig into the ways we need to work together in Tactic 9. Key Results are the are the most important outcomes that ultimately define our success.

Each Key Result should accomplish the three Ms: They should be Meaningful, Memorable, and Measurable.

Measurable: Each Key Result should be measurable. For most results, there's no perfect metric. Just ask your CFO how many different ways they can measure profitability. Just pick the best one. It could be a revenue figure or growth percentage. It could be a customer satisfaction metric or an employee engagement percentage. Don't spend months or even weeks debating the perfect metric. It doesn't exist.

Meaningful: The three Key Results you land on should be ambitious enough to motivate people and generate discussion. The three categories you choose send a message about how you as a leader define success and what you care about most. Everyone should be able to connect how they impact each of these three Key Results. Some people will have a direct impact; others, an indirect impact.

Memorable: Try to land on words or metrics that are sticky. Easy to remember. We've seen a large food manufacturer end up with: 5/10/1. Each one of those numbers was tied to a specific result that thousands of employees were working toward and aware of. We worked with a global vehicle manufacturer to identify the Three Zeros. Within months, frontline union employees in plants throughout the world could tell you what the Three Zeros meant. That phenomenon resulted from a single principle: memorability.

The Key Results create alignment for individuals working from different locations to achieve the same results. What they do should help move the team closer to achieving those Key Results. If you're the leader of a team and the Key Results of the organization haven't been communicated down the org chart to you, don't let that stop you from creating them for your team. Don't let a lack of clarity from your boss cause you to not create clarity on what matters most for *your* team. We've seen countless leaders elevated in their organizations or industries because they didn't fall victim to a lack of clarity in other parts of their company. Instead, they took accountability for accelerating results.

We share additional examples of what Key Results look like in the free online training videos that accompany this book at **remoteabilitybook.com.**

NEXT, BE CLEAR ON KEY EXPECTATIONS

Key Results help direct your team to work on the right things. When you can't see and interact with your team members as often, it's critical they have clarity not just on the Key Results but also on what we call Key Expectations.

Key Expectations are those things you need people doing in the next 90 days.

In the weeks immediately following the discovery of Covid-19 spreading inside the United States, Tanner was on the phone with "Mike", the head of sales for a division of a food manufacturing company. Mike's division had hundreds of sales reps spread out across the country. Their primary customers were universities, hotels, and restaurants.

Think back to those early days of the pandemic and the impact on university campuses, on the travel industry, and on restaurants. All three became ghost towns. Suddenly, Mike's division, which was crushing their year-to-date results at the time, was dealing with massive disruption and uncertainty.

They had warehouses producing tons of meat and food products ready to be shipped to customers who were suddenly cancelling their orders. In that first call with Mike after the pandemic hit, he sounded exactly how you'd expect: deeply concerned. "We have a saying in this business that if you don't sell the product, you smell the product," Mike said.

Tanner asked, "Is your team clear on what you expect them to be doing right now?" After some discussion, he realized they probably weren't. Kicking off a meeting on Zoom with the entire sales force, Mike announced the Key Expectation of "5 by 25." He explained that he needed every sales rep to contact 5 potential customers who had never done business with the company by the twenty-fifth day of the next month. Within minutes, hundreds of Mike's sales reps had clarity on what they needed to do starting immediately.

A Key Expectation is the most important short-term expectation, where you realize not delivering is *not* an option. Key Expectations not only tell people what to do; they also tell people what to stop doing.

We recommend having no more than three Key Expectations at a time. They should cover what you need people focused on for the next 90 days that will help deliver the Key Results.

History teaches that humans want to follow honesty and integrity, but *they will* follow clarity. Even the vilest of causes throughout time has gained traction because the direction offered by the leader of the movement was crystal clear.

Remoteability begins by being clear on what you need your team to deliver and helping them focus on what they should be doing in the coming weeks to achieve those results.

NEXT STEPS

▶ Get clear with your team on 3 Key Results for the next 12 months (category and metric for each one).

▶ Get clear with your team on 1–3 Key Expectations for the next 60–90 days (and make them memorable, like "5 by 25").

- -

GENERATE ALIGNMENT

- -

12 TACTICS

1. CREATE CLARITY
2. GENERATE ALIGNMENT
3. BUILD ACCOUNTABILITY
4. BE VISIBLE
5. BE ACCESSIBLE
6. BE TRANSPARENT
7. INCREASE AGILITY
8. DEMONSTRATE EMPATHY
9. MANAGE BELIEFS
10. RUN EFFECTIVE MEETINGS
11. VALIDATE AUTHENTICITY
12. ENSURE WELL-BEING

Now that you've got clarity around the Key Expectations and Key Results, you can just sit back and watch the magic happen, right? We wish! Clarity doesn't guarantee alignment. Far from it. Just because you've created a beautiful PowerPoint slide announcing the three Key Results in an emotional, inspiring way doesn't mean you've eradicated questions, concerns, and even doubts.

Ryan is the CEO of a manufacturing company that quickly adapted some of their products to meet changing consumer demands in the first few months after Covid-19 hit. In our monthly call with him, he shared how proud he was of the thousands of his employees who changed how they worked, literally overnight. That's good enough, right? Nope. Along with the excitement we felt from him was a deep concern. Ryan put it like this: "I hope we don't think we've done enough. We need to innovate like this all the time now. It's who we have to be if we're going to keep growing market share."

The company had to view themselves as innovators. Honestly, they have thousands of operators and hundreds of managers who know the ins and outs of the busines better than anyone. They needed to constantly drive change to improve speed-to-market. We brought the topic into the next virtual meeting. We split the expanded leadership team into breakout rooms and gave each team 10 minutes to agree on an Innovation Score for the company.

Ryan waited with us for the teams to come back to the "main room" of the virtual meeting and report out. He needed to know if his definition of innovation matched theirs. He needed to know if this team understood how critical being a disruptive force in their industry was. He needed to hear the obstacles that people perceived in increasing speed-to-market.

The meeting agenda was designed to measure alignment and to create more of it. Having your vehicle's tires aligned assures alignment only up until you hit the next pothole. Ryan knew that Covid-19 was a massive pothole and they were hitting it at 75 miles an hour. He was smart to slow down and not assume alignment but to pressure check it instead.

ALIGNMENT ISN'T AWARENESS

Just because your team is aware of something rarely means they're aligned to it. Before Covid, we regularly stood in the back of ballrooms and watched leaders on the stage mistake silence, head nods, or even applause for alignment. When some people applaud next year's sales target, it's only because they have a mortgage and don't want to fail the IQ test they just found themselves taking! It's not likely because they think you picked the right number or because they believe it can be achieved.

 The truth is your team has questions, concerns, and objections about the Key Results.

Most employees don't vocalize those in meetings—especially virtual meetings—because they aren't sure how you as the leader are going to respond. Will you misinterpret their questions as a bad attitude? So, they save the questions and concerns for texts or calls to coworkers after the meeting.

Making your team aware of the Key Results is the starting point, but there's much more to be done to create alignment. Awareness does not equal alignment. Teams that are aware of a result or expectation perform very differently from teams that are aligned around an expectation or result.

The challenge is most of our virtual meetings are designed to create awareness, not alignment. One person does most of the talking. Others are leaning back listening or multi-tasking rather than contributing. Information is shared but not discussed, very few questions are asked, and the silence speaks volumes. Alignment *sounds* much different. It's noisy. It's messy. Leaders seeking alignment ask questions and lean into debate and pushback as part of the natural process leading to alignment. A meeting seeking alignment looks like what we described above as Ryan sought to measure and create alignment with his expanded leadership team around innovation.

ALIGNMENT ISN'T AGREEMENT

Another distinction we need to make is around the words "alignment" and "agreement." Alignment is an agreement to move in the same direction, regardless of whether or not I think there's a better way forward. Leaders who fail to properly define and communicate this definition of alignment tend to waste a lot of energy trying to gain agreement. Leaders shouldn't seek agreement or full consensus from the team. They need to seek alignment—or an agreement to move forward in the same direction. That's what's needed!

For years we've watched teams struggle to make decisions. Some leaders want everyone to feel good about the direction they need to go, and work to achieve complete consensus before moving ahead. This approach leads to lots of redundant discussion, analysis paralysis, lost time, frustration and a false sense of agreement, as team members give up out of exhaustion. Working in a virtual environment only makes this worse. After hours and hours on Zoom or Team meetings, the last thing many of us want is more time in some meeting trying to agree on something. Try getting a group of people to agree on anything! It rarely happens.

For a group to make a decision, you need consensus. Any one person can derail or delay the process for any number of reasons, even personal ones that may not be what's best for the team or organization. Alignment almost always requires some members of the team to set aside their own opinions or preferences for the good of the team.

THE DECISION MAP

So, how do you create alignment? What does that process look like when you're leading a virtual or hybrid team? We recommend a simple framework for decision-making that efficiently creates alignment throughout your team. We suggest you use this process when you're rolling out Key Results, Key Expectations, a new project, or policy.

We call this the Decision Map. It's four steps that lead you to the best decision possible while concurrently instilling ownership in each team member. Each step has a question or two associated with it.

Step One: Define
What decision needs to be made?
Who is the decision-maker?

How often have you been in a meeting and wondered: What are we actually doing in this meeting? What decision needs to be made? Or, who is the decision-maker for this particular decision? Groups don't make decisions; they're terrible at it. Leaders make decisions. Teams inform leaders so they make the *best* decision.

Next time you log in to a meeting and you don't know what the decision is that this meeting is designed to help make or who the decision-maker is, speak up! Ask for clarity on both.

The decision-maker is often the most senior person involved in the discussion but not always. Some decisions should be delegated. Move decision-making as close to the customer as you can, and you'll see those decisions more positively impact results.

Step One: Define

Step Two: Discuss

Have the appropriate people been heard?

Involvement leads to ownership. Leaders often wonder why people aren't taking accountability for a policy, result, or decision. The reason is often because they feel their perspective wasn't considered in the process that led to the policy change, the result they're now told to deliver, or the decision that affects how they do their work.

When you're making a decision that you need people to take accountability for, consider two groups of people: 1) those who can best inform you so you make the best decision possible, and 2) those who will be expected to implement or be affected by the decision. Invite representatives of both groups to be part of the discussion you facilitate before making the decision.

Some of us err on the side of inviting too many people to the discussion. Others lean toward not enough. Be aware of your tendencies here and strike the sweet spot between the two. The two measures of decisions are speed and quality. Achieving one while ignoring the other leads to poor decisions.

Allow time for enough discussion. Make a point of asking those who don't readily offer their perspectives in meetings or digital conversations to speak up. Sometimes their silence is due to a crushing workload keeping them from fully understanding the details. Often, it's due to apathy. Beware of the latter, and combat it by not listening just to the extroverts.

To further the discussion, it's a best practice to ask this question of the participants you've invited: "Do you feel heard?" Don't wait until you've already communicated the new direction only to find that your chief of staff has been running around telling everyone they can't believe the decision was made without understanding a critical piece of information. Ask the question before you make the decision.

As a leader, it's important to move the discussion along by taking positions periodically, allowing the team to react. You may say something like, "If I had to make the decision on this now, I'm inclined to go this direction. Am I missing something?" Taking a position tells the team where you're leaning and allows them a chance to convince you you've lost your mind and are about to make a massive mistake. In other words, speak now or forever hold your peace because this rocket is about to take off.

Step One: Define

Step Two: Discuss

Step Three: Decide

What's the decision?

Once everyone has been heard, it's time to make the decision. If you're the decision-maker, this step is as simple and clear as announcing your decision. If you're not the decision-maker but were part of the discussion, you should call for the decision once everyone has been heard.

Our experience is decisions rarely improve when they're delayed. A good vs great decision is often better than no decision. Decisions provide clarity, focus, collaboration, and movement. Indecision leads to confusion, poor execution, wasted resources, and delay.

We're fans of Amazon's leadership principle called Bias for Action. The definition Jeff Bezos and his S-Team wrote for the principle is:

 Speed matters in business. Many decisions and actions are reversible and do not need extensive study. We value calculated risk taking.

Every Amazonian is expected to memorize that leadership principle and adhere to it. Think of the impact that has on speed-to-market and agility inside the tech company's culture!

Step One: Define

Step Two: Discuss

Step Three: Decide

Step Four: Own

Will you own the decision as if you made it yourself?

Nothing destroys alignment more than someone logging out of a meeting and then actively seeking to sabotage it. They say things like, "I spoke up against that decision in our meeting," or "I can't believe they made that decision; I told them it wasn't going to work." Leaders should make it clear that they're not seeking agreement with their decisions but rather alignment with them. We put people in positions of leadership to make decisions. If we've been given a chance to offer our opinion and insight, that's all we can ask for as decisions are considered.

Own the decision as if you made it yourself!

As you announce the decision, whether you made it or not, make sure you communicate the process followed to reach the decision. Often those reading about the decision in an email or hearing it announced in a meeting will align quicker when they learn their perspective was represented in the process leading to that decision. It's also very important to clearly describe the "why" behind the decision.

NEXT STEPS

▶ Evaluate a recent decision you made through the lens of the four steps of the Decision Map. What one or two steps did you execute well? What one or two steps could you have done more effectively?

▶ Identify an upcoming decision, project, or policy change, and map out how you will follow the four steps outlined above to create alignment.

BUILD ACCOUNTABILITY

---

12 TACTICS

1. CREATE CLARITY
2. GENERATE ALIGNMENT
3. **BUILD ACCOUNTABILITY**
4. BE VISIBLE
5. BE ACCESSIBLE
6. BE TRANSPARENT
7. INCREASE AGILITY
8. DEMONSTRATE EMPATHY
9. MANAGE BELIEFS
10. RUN EFFECTIVE MEETINGS
11. VALIDATE AUTHENTICITY
12. ENSURE WELL-BEING

Tanner and his wife Erin filmed a conversation with their daughter a number of years ago that has since been viewed by millions of people. Noelle, their not-quite-three-year-old daughter, had developed a habit of seeing their furniture as a blank canvas for her artistic impulses. No piece of furniture was safe from this blooming Picasso. Perhaps you've had a kid who liked writing on furniture or walls as well. You know how much it can drive you crazy!

After being caught in the act by her older sister, Tanner and Erin approached Noelle about her latest masterpiece. This time, she had taken a pencil to the kitchen chairs. Their iPhone captured this priceless exchange:

> *Tanner: "Noelle, who drew on the chair?"*
> *Noelle, already beginning to hunker down to the ground: "I was coloring on the table and saw Lily do it."*
> *Tanner: "Lily did it? Are you sure?"*
> *Noelle: "Yeah, Lily did it."*
> *Tanner: "But how is that possible? Lily is only eight months old."*
> *Noelle: "She did it."*
> *Tanner: "Hmmm. Okay. What should we do to Lily?"*
> *Noelle: "She should be in trouble!"*
> *Tanner: "Okay. We'll go talk to Lily if you're sure it wasn't you."*
> *Noelle, now curled into a full-fetal position: "No. It wasn't me."*

The video then scans over to baby Lily, sleeping soundly in her bassinet, innocent as a lamb and barely old enough to keep a binky in her mouth.

> *To view this hilarious video visit the website that accompanies this book at* **remoteabilitybook.com.**

Where does a three-year-old child learn how to blame like that? Tanner would tell you that they learn it from their mothers. Brave man. *(We all know the truth, Erin!)*

 Have you ever worked with, or been related to, someone who makes excuses for everything? Someone who spends much of their time blaming unborn generations for their problems?

Or have you ever seen your phone ringing, looked at the caller ID, and thought to yourself, "Oh no. How much time am I about to lose?" because on the other end of that call is a never-ending story of victimization? Everyone naturally spends some time feeling victimized by other people or external circumstances. The question is, how much time do you spend there?

Teams can suffer from the same tendency. We were once in a client meeting where *every person* in the room was blaming their production team in China for defects in one of their medical device pumps. The reflex to "blame China" had become so commonplace that you could blame China for a dirty kitchen fridge at the US headquarters and everyone would readily agree with you. In this particular meeting, we thought we'd challenge the "blame China for everything" narrative. So we said, "Are we really blaming China for not delivering on our revenue plan again this year?" One woman quickly responded, "Yes! I'm blaming all one billion of them!" Wow. I guess if it worked last year...

Thankfully, most teams aren't like that, but in moments of disruption and uncertainty it's easier than ever to play the blame game. As a leader of a remote team, you need people taking accountability for delivering results while refusing to spend time focused on things they can't control.

Here's one of your challenges: How many members of your team would raise their hand in response to the following question: "Are you an accountable person?" Every single hand would go up, right? If you ask the same group to raise their hand if they think more accountability is needed on the team or in the organization, every hand goes up again. That's the paradox! We all think we're personally accountable and yet we need more accountability on our team. So, who's the problem? Clearly not me!

THE DEFINITION OF ACCOUNTABILITY

We should probably get aligned on what the word "account-ability" even means. The word itself can feel pretty heavy-handed. Schedule a meeting titled "Creating Greater Account-ability," and see how many people can't wait to attend. Not many, right? That's because, typically, accountability is a word that comes up when things go south. When results aren't delivered. When targets are missed. Here's a better defini-tion to consider.

 Accountability: a personal choice to focus on what you can control or impact, to demonstrate ownership for achieving the Key Results.

As your team works in new and different ways and in an envi-ronment of significant changes in customer expectations, resource availability, and more uncertainty than ever, it's easy for them to focus on what they can't control.

They can have the most accountable mindset, and suddenly a notification pings their phone with an update from their kid's school, new restrictions in their city or state, or a cus-tomer changing their mind, and suddenly they slip into The Excuse Zone. Their entire focus shifts to a new obstacle. It consumes them for hours or even days.

EXCUSES ARE HUMAN NATURE

Don't get us wrong. It's absolutely normal—and human—to focus on obstacles and things out of our control. We're not suggesting that you expect your team to never fall into The Excuse Zone. In fact, we coach leaders all the time to anticipate and tolerate members of their team losing focus and surrendering to the uncertainty and obstacles they encounter. There's nothing wrong with doing that—as long as it's temporary. It's not wrong to fall into The Excuse Zone. It is wrong to get stuck there.

Tom Smith, our friend and co-author of the *New York Times* bestseller *The Oz Principle*, made the following comment to us during a conversation in the moments right after Covid-19 hit.

> *"In any given moment of life, you can choose pessimism, and there's all sorts of justification to make that choice. But that pessimism does not breed innovation, resolution, or opportunity, and so I resist the pessimistic viewpoint."*

He's right. Focusing on the obstacle for a moment and venting about it is human nature. It's even therapeutic. We should allow our team members to express that frustration in moments following changes in policies, resources, systems, or demand. Great leaders don't overreact to temporary expression of excuses and blame. They shouldn't, however, tolerate someone on the team who becomes permanently stuck, blaming nonperformance on everyone or everything else around them.

We saw this play out in a virtual meeting with a global company we work with. They made changes to their structure and announced them in an email. People in the impacted departments felt disappointed, confused, and even misled in some cases. We had a virtual meeting scheduled with members of the team a few days after the changes were announced.

As we began facilitating the virtual meeting, it became clear that more than half the employees logged in were not in a mindset of taking accountability. They had very little interest in talking about how to accelerate achieving results. They just needed to vent about the changes. We threw out our agenda for the meeting and provided a venue for as many of them as possible to be heard over the next 90 minutes or so.

We've learned that you have to let people vent about obstacles before you can expect them to make a choice to focus on what they control. That meeting helped clear the air. It had a powerful impact on the culture of that part of the company.

MODEL THE BEHAVIOR YOU NEED

As you seek to create an environment of accountability on your team, the best way to generate movement is to model the behavior you want others to demonstrate. A powerful way to do that in your next virtual meeting with your team is to share an obstacle that temporarily derailed you in the last couple of weeks. That obstacle could be a new policy sent down from corporate. It could be a disruption in the supply chain. It could be a customer changing their order, or even something that happened with your kid's school changing from in-person back to online learning.

Start your next meeting sharing a 1–2 minute story of how this obstacle caused you to lose your focus, the emotion you felt because of it, and the effort you had to make to get back in the game and focus on what you control in your effort to deliver the Key Results. Then, quickly acknowledge that your team is dealing with the same kinds of obstacles and express appreciation to them for not allowing these obstacles to derail them from working on delivering the Key Results.

This simple act has a profound impact on a team's culture. It communicates that you're human. It signals to the rest of the team that you understand and are empathetic to the challenge they're having staying focused while working at home and in this uncertain environment. You telling that story authorizes everyone else to acknowledge the obstacles they're dealing with. It also shows them that the goal here is to not allow the things they can't control to derail them.

 Teams develop narratives around results. When they're not careful, leaders turn obstacles into valid reasons for not delivering the Key Results.

Your team might even have its own version of "Blame China." It's important to identify those narratives and to challenge them head on. Your words matter. Don't pretend the obstacles don't exist. Acknowledge them with empathy, but make it clear they aren't justification for not achieving the Key Results. How you talk about these challenges your team is experiencing plays a major role in whether they become an obstacle that is being overcome or the accepted excuse for why targets will be missed.

Taking accountability is all about staying focused on the needed results and working through the obstacles that will always pop up along the way. It's about avoiding the natural tendency to do nothing, and justifying it by the fact that it's not your fault. Results come when you take action driven by ownership of the needed outcome.

Accountability is contagious. The more you demonstrate and call it out when you see it the more it will be the mindset of your team.

NEXT STEPS

► Teach your team the definition of accountability shared in this chapter.

► Frequently share examples with your team of where you, and they, have resisted the urge to fall into The Excuse Zone and instead chosen to focus on what you control.

► Be aware of the narrative that's developing on your team around the Key Results. Make sure obstacles are being overcome rather than becoming the accepted excuses for not hitting your targets.

Tactic 4

BE VISIBLE

- -

12 TACTICS

1. CREATE CLARITY
2. GENERATE ALIGNMENT
3. BUILD ACCOUNTABILITY
4. BE VISIBLE
5. BE ACCESSIBLE
6. BE TRANSPARENT
7. INCREASE AGILITY
8. DEMONSTRATE EMPATHY
9. MANAGE BELIEFS
10. RUN EFFECTIVE MEETINGS
11. VALIDATE AUTHENTICITY
12. ENSURE WELL-BEING

When terrorists struck the United States of America on
September 11, 2001, President George W. Bush was visiting an elementary school in Sarasota, Florida. His advis-
ers whisked him to an empty classroom, where they were
able to connect him with his national security team. Once
he grasped the magnitude of the moment, he immediately
sought out television cameras. He wanted to do one thing
immediately: be visible to the American people.

In moments of uncertainty, disruption, and change, leaders
must increase their visibility—visibility to their teams, their
boss, and their customers. A lack of visibility typically leads
to people filling the silence with worst-case speculation and
conspiracy theories. People sense the leadership void and
go into full stop mode or run wild doing anything to be busy
with no focus or direction (like a six-year-old watching ants
scurry after dropping a rock on an ant hill). Neither of those
reactions, full stop or scurry mode, help achieve the desired
results. Increased visibility creates stability, direction, and
alignment.

THE WALMART EXAMPLE

One of the organizations we work with is led by a CEO who
clearly understands the value of visibility. As most places
were locking down amid a tremendous amount of uncertainty and fear around Covid-19, Walmart's Doug McMillon
made the decision to increase his visibility. He got out of his
office and hit the road. Every day for weeks, he visited a store

somewhere in America. He posted pictures and brief stories of his visits to his social media accounts including LinkedIn.

Doug McMillon 🔗 · Following
President & CEO at Walmart Inc.
6mo · 🌐   · · ·

Out and about in Temple, TX, today and I'm pleased to report our toilet paper in-stock is improving! John Furner and I enjoyed visiting with Eulalio and Megan at Store 746 as well as the team at Sam's Club 6336!

👍👏💚 6,128 · 207 Comments

After just a brief moment of looking at one of the pictures, you got the message: Walmart stores are open for business and Doug McMillon is in charge and steering the way. It put Doug on the front line of his company and directly inter-acting with customers more than ever as he faced a slew of decisions about what Walmart would do to respond to the pandemic. Instead of making the decisions from his isolated corporate headquarter office, he was issuing them from a position of being trusted by those asked to implement them.

Visibility is critical in moments of disruption and uncer-tainty, but it's also critical in more mundane times for leaders of remote teams. It's rare for someone in a shared workspace to go very long without seeing other members of the team or you, their leader. But, in a work-from-home environment, it can be several days sometimes between conversations with members of the team. The longer you, as the leader of the team, go without interacting with your teammates the greater the odds are that they'll lose focus on the Key Results, be distracted by other projects or requests, or fall out of alignment with recent decisions you've made.

After surveying more than 1,200 employees working from home during 2020, researchers at Harvard made the following observation:

> "Sometimes managers confuse autonomy with abdication or abandonment of employees. Managers need to learn that autonomy doesn't mean less communication with employees. But rather than checking up on people as a way to micromanage them, managers need to check in with people and provide them the information, guidance, and support to work autonomously."

Visibility is one way. It's controlled entirely by you. You determine how much your team, your boss, and your customers see and hear from you. The driving force behind your visibility is to bring stability, to give direction, and to create alignment. It helps your team stay focused, and it helps you have peace of mind that they're working on what matters most.

INCREASING YOUR VISIBILITY

When you're leading a remote team, you have to be much more intentional about being visible. Frequency and authenticity of your interactions are at the heart of how visible you are. Without effort by you, members of your team could easily go days without seeing you. An absence of visibility by a leader almost always leads to a lack of alignment and focus by the team.

Based on best practices of visibility we've seen by leaders of remote teams, we recommend you:

Increase the number of touch points with your team members to make up for the lack of interaction and conversations that used to happen in shared office space. *Increasing the frequency of one-on-ones and other team meetings should be balanced by decreasing the length of them.*

Increase the number of touch points with your boss and peers. They need to see and hear from you. Take accountability for texting them, and call them every day or two. Don't wait until they ping you! You'll know what the right cadence is for different people you report to or work with.

Turn your camera on in your virtual meetings. People need to not just hear you. They need to see you. Keep it on, even when you're not speaking. Your team will be watching your body language as you listen to others during meetings.

Increase the number of informal calls you make to members of your team. Reach out to them more than you did before they were remote. Check in to see what questions they have, what obstacles they're running into, what progress they're making toward the Key Results and Key Expectations.

Demonstrate empathy by inquiring about their family and personal life. Spend at least five minutes connecting as a friend before digging into the work.

Increase your presence on company communication or project management portals like Slack or Asana. Make comments. Post questions. Make your presence known so people are aware that you're connected to them and their work.

Send or post recognition more frequently for behavior you want repeated. These are the sorts of comments you would have made in the hallway, break room, or parking garage when you saw someone who did something noteworthy. Recognizing that kind of positive behavior requires more intentionality and effort when leading a virtual team.

Send quick texts to team members to check how their day is going or to share a quick motivational thought or success.

Visibility has two other parts to it critical to helping your remote team deliver the Key Results. We decided that rather than write a long chapter about all three, we'd split them up and give them each individual focus and attention in separate chapters. Those two other aspects of visibility are transparency and accessibility. We've learned from watching our clients that increasing visibility is critical but not enough to promote the agility and accountability needed for delivering Key Results in an environment of constant change including working remotely. We'll dive into transparency and accessibility next.

NEXT STEPS

▶ Look at your weekly calendar and ask: "Am I visible enough to my team?"

▶ Select a few ideas from the list above and implement them this week.

- -

BE ACCESSIBLE

---

12 TACTICS

1. CREATE CLARITY
2. GENERATE ALIGNMENT
3. BUILD ACCOUNTABILITY
4. BE VISIBLE
5. BE ACCESSIBLE
6. BE TRANSPARENT
7. INCREASE AGILITY
8. DEMONSTRATE EMPATHY
9. MANAGE BELIEFS
10. RUN EFFECTIVE MEETINGS
11. VALIDATE AUTHENTICITY
12. ENSURE WELL-BEING

Being visible is critically important, but it has major limitations if you're not also accessible. Part of the reason we divided Tactics 4, 5 and 6 into different chapters is because we wanted to impress upon you how each of these tactics are related and yet vital on their own as well.

As we discussed in the last chapter, visibility is you making yourself present. It's outward communication. Accessibility is you making yourself available. It's how you handle inward communication.

One of the national restaurant chains we work with had a national conference back when those were still happening. The event allowed the company's new CEO to introduce himself to thousands of store managers who had flown in from across the United States. We were getting ready for our turn on the stage when he did something that we had never seen before. He asked all 4,000 store managers to get out their cell phones. Then, on the huge screen behind him, he put up his personal cell phone number.

"If you need me, now you know how to get ahold of me," he said. The room erupted in applause. Why? Because that experience led to a belief. The belief he wanted all of those leaders to absorb was he was going to be accessible.

ACCESSIBILITY CREATES SPEED

Leaders are paid to make decisions. That's a huge part of your role no matter where you sit in the organization. Your team seeks you out when customers, patients, members, partners, or colleagues have questions and need a decision to be made. Think what happens when they can't get hold of you. Everything slows to a crawl. Uncertainty abounds. Alignment starts to break down. Customers get frustrated.

In a shared workspace, accessibility looks like an open office door. You don't have to put much effort into being accessible in that environment. People know how to find you if they need you. In a remote work environment, your team can't see you most of the day. They don't know what you're doing. And yet they still need your perspectives and insight and decisions.

 When they text you and it takes hours for you to respond, everything slows down. When emails go unanswered, progress toward results is stalled.

Roger Connors, a co-founder of the firm Partners In Leadership, used to be our boss. He is one of the busiest people we've ever encountered. The man moves at warp speed and gets more done in a single day than most of us get done in a week. And yet we were constantly surprised that 99% of the time we called Roger's phone he immediately answered. Sometimes he answered just long enough to say he'd call us back later. Everyone in our company held a belief that if you called Roger he would pick up. Roger was accessible. That accelerated the speed of our company.

It's not just others who benefit from your accessibility. It also increases your value. The more accessible you are to those closest to the customer the more insight and value you bring to the organization. Being accessible opens up channels of communication that enable you to offer innovative solutions and important adjustments to policies and systems that stimulate growth. It helps build a habit of getting things done today rather than putting it off or scheduling the conversation in the future. It helps you become a "doer."

THERE ARE EXCEPTIONS

We wanted to make sure we validated placing some limits on your accessibility. As much as we champion accessibility, we're also huge believers in having a family-first mindset. All three of us have families of six people or more. We're also active in our faith and communities. As much as we love consulting and coaching leaders around the world, we love being with our families more. We like to say of all the places we've traveled around the globe our favorite destination is home.

 Being accessible shouldn't come at the expense of the people we live with or are related to. The way to make sure this family time doesn't slow down the organization or your team is to define and interpret when you won't be accessible.

In a remote work environment, this is essential. People can't see if your office light is off and the door is closed. They don't know when you're "on the clock," so to speak. Leading a remote team demands, where possible, we let people know in advance when we won't be accessible, and we identify a backup so day-to-day decisions can proceed without us.

NEXT STEPS

▶ Consider how accessible you are to your team. Seek their feedback about it.

▶ Make appropriate adjustments so customers, employees, and colleagues develop a belief that you're available when they need you.

- -

BE TRANSPARENT

---

12 TACTICS

1. CREATE CLARITY
2. GENERATE ALIGNMENT
3. BUILD ACCOUNTABILITY
4. BE VISIBLE
5. BE ACCESSIBLE
6. BE TRANSPARENT
7. INCREASE AGILITY
8. DEMONSTRATE EMPATHY
9. MANAGE BELIEFS
10. RUN EFFECTIVE MEETINGS
11. VALIDATE AUTHENTICITY
12. ENSURE WELL-BEING

Once you've made yourself more visible and accessible, now comes the most important step of these three related tactics: being transparent.

 What good is visibility or accessibility if people don't trust the information you're sharing with them?

A large food manufacturing company we consult has been plagued with all kinds of challenges in their supply chain during the Covid-19 pandemic. Grocery stores rely on them to supply products for their deli departments and meat counters. Social distancing restrictions have dramatically cut their factory output, and supplies they rely upon have just not been available.

This has led to fury among their customers. Senior leaders of large grocery chains have berated them on phone call after phone call. Our client has worked hard to be visible to these customers and to be accessible. All of that would have done very little good if they weren't transparent. These leaders have provided all kinds of data and insight on why they're unable to get the requested volume to their customers. They've owned failures and mistakes that their teams have been responsible for, and they've resisted the urge to make excuses but instead have focused on creative solutions.

The transparency doesn't remove the frustration the grocery store chains have in the moment, but it has definitely preserved the relationships. A lack of transparency at any moment in these conversations would likely sever the partnership.

For the next few pages, we will offer recommendations on how to ensure transparency rules the day. Without conscious effort to cement these lessons, many could miss the benefits created by this sea change.

THE TRANSPARENCY FALLACIES

Let's first address the fallacies that influence a lack of transparency:

Fallacy #1:

"I don't want to create unnecessary panic or fear in the culture, so I'm not going to communicate too much information."

Today's workforce cannot only handle transparency but demands it. The human resources policies of the past need to be just that. Yes, people's privacy should be protected and some information can't be shared, but it's our belief that many leaders conceal far more than they need to using the "confidentiality" excuse. The truth eventually comes out. When it does, the first question on everyone's minds is, "How long has our leader known about this?" There are, of course, instances where too much transparency, too early, can do harm. But don't adopt the exception as your rule!

Fallacy #2:

"Information is power, and I lose power when I share too much."

A lie detector might be needed to discover this mindset in most of us, but it does exist and it does nothing but separate a leader from the team. If information is power, ensure you're empowering your team.

Fallacy #3:

"My people already have a good sense of what I'm thinking."

We overestimate how well we are communicating our feelings and thoughts. When we are frustrated or nervous or angry, we falsely assume that anyone who looks at us can mindread. The fact is that our poker face is much better than we realize. Thoughts and emotions are yours and only yours until they're communicated openly.

Decades worth of client data has taught us team members who spend time questioning whether they're getting the whole story from their leaders are less engaged and tend to not collaborate as much. They lack trust. When team members feel like they have the full picture, even if that picture is one of hot lava chasing them towards a cliff, at least the team knows what the future holds and can act accordingly. Not knowing is worse! Working remotely makes this situation worse. It creates more uncertainty, which breeds suspicion.

Ninety percent of leaders say increased business transparency leads to better-informed decision-making across the entire organization *(Harvard Business Review Analytic Services Study 2020).*

That's a staggering number of leaders who agree on the need for more transparency... in principle. Unfortunately, many leaders aren't demonstrating this in practice. According to our firm's research involving over 40,000 employees of companies all over the world, only 8% of employees strongly agree that transparency exists across the organization when it comes to important initiatives. That's a sobering commentary stating that most employees feel left in the dark about what matters most in their organization.

Netflix's former Chief Talent Officer Patty McCord advocates "treating employees like adults." She calls transparency "radical honesty." She shared with us the story of a meeting she held with Netflix employees the day after the company laid off hundreds of people. This was during their formative years. She stood on a chair the morning after the layoffs and said, "We are not your family," and that the cutbacks "were necessary" and would "help the company be stronger." McCord was revered at the company for her straight talk.

WHAT TRANSPARENCY LOOKS LIKE

You'll know transparency is working when teams frequently ask the right questions. When transparency is missing, teams go silent. Whenever we see silence or the absence of questions when leaders call for them, we know there's room for improved transparency.

One of the largest manufacturing companies in the world has 14 plants in the United States. One of those plants is in the Midwest and was at the bottom of the list in production output, cost per case, and safety. Strangely, employees at the plant actually thought they were doing just fine.

A brand new chief operating officer visited the plant and presented a picture of a completely rusted out VW Bug covered in brush and leaves with a tree growing up through its floor and out the roof. He said, "This is how the senior leadership team in Massachusetts sees you at this plant."

Everyone present that day remembers well the message that was shared in that meeting. It was sobering transparency but totally necessary to create the needed change. Without "radical honesty" about the plant's performance, the team would have done little to change. Every witness to that day also remembers the next 18 months. Significant improvements followed within weeks as the team became laser-focused on closing the gap in output and efficiency. Just over a year after the VW picture was burned into their memories, the team celebrated breaking into the top three spots of all 14 plants on production and safety metrics. Transparency creates movement.

As you combine the last three tactics—visibility, accessibility, and transparency—something special happens. When leaders compound their efforts to be visible with greater accessibility and transparency, performance improves. You ultimately get execution at greater speed!

For more on the connection between visibility, accessibility, and transparency and how they affect the speed and agility of a team view the video on this topic at **remoteabilitybook.com.**

NEXT STEPS

▶ What details could be shared with your team that you are currently not speaking about? If you would share those details with each member of your team one on one, why can't you share it with them as a team?

▶ Where do you need more speed? How can you use visibility, accessibility and transparency to create additional pace?

INCREASE AGILITY

- -

12 TACTICS

1. CREATE CLARITY
2. GENERATE ALIGNMENT
3. BUILD ACCOUNTABILITY
4. BE VISIBLE
5. BE ACCESSIBLE
6. BE TRANSPARENT
7. INCREASE AGILITY
8. DEMONSTRATE EMPATHY
9. MANAGE BELIEFS
10. RUN EFFECTIVE MEETINGS
11. VALIDATE AUTHENTICITY
12. ENSURE WELL-BEING

Want to see agility? Look at any parent who has had to become principal of the new online learning academy based in their home! Jared has six children, aged from first grade up to college. When in-person classes got shifted to home, agility wasn't an option for him and his wife, Christy.

Everyone needed access to a computer or tablet. Couches were removed. Make-shift desks were created. Wi-Fi was upgraded. And strict new rules about headphones and noise level took effect. Oh... and ask Jared about the once-a-week PE class he now teaches for the elementary school kids in his neighborhood! *(Jared teaching PE almost made this book fiction, but we've seen the pictures. It actually happened.)*

Any of you who have kids in school know how much flexibility and agility the last year has required. Agility is a word we've heard a ton in the last few years, but it might be a good idea to define it.

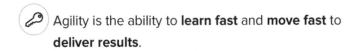 Agility is the ability to **learn fast** and **move fast** to **deliver results**.

Most of us don't like change. It's hardwired into our DNA to find the path of least resistance. To be agile means to confront that fact and push past it.

LESSONS FROM INTEL'S ANDY GROVE

One of the champions of agility and innovation in the modern tech age was Andrew Grove. He helped Intel become the powerhouse it's been for the last several decades. Grove did it by developing leaders into skilled managers of team culture. Something he said toward the end of his tenure at Intel stands out to us.

> *"Every company faces a critical point when it must change dramatically to rise to the next level of performance. If the company fails to see and seize that moment, it will start to decline. The key is courage,"* Grove said.

Think how many companies are at that critical point right now. How often do we look externally for someone to drive the change Grove mentioned? The reality is those best suited to drive change are those closest to the customer. As we look up the org chart for direction, we tend to see executives looking back at us, hoping we will lead the change. It's interesting to us that Grove said the "key is courage." Why courage?

Perhaps it's because the defenders of the status quo have sharp claws. They don't go down easily. Perhaps we're waiting for someone else to lead the change and provide us cover and *perceived* protection. Maybe it's because we're not 100% confident our ideas will be embraced or even work.

Agility does demand courage. Taking risks and trying new things will lead to some mistakes and poor decisions. But which group would you rather be in during this age of change? The group that's paralyzed by change (the 90% in the Panic and Stunned Modes), or those out creating the solutions for the future (the 10%)?

CUSTOMERS ARE DEMANDING CHANGE

Harvard Business School professor Thales Teixeira spent eight years visiting companies in more than 20 industries. Every single company claimed to be disrupted. This was before 2020! Teixeira said she asked executives at every company to identify the source of disruption. "No matter who I talked to, I would always get one of two answers: 'Technology X is disrupting our business' or 'Startup Y is disrupting our business,'" Teixeira reported.

She wrote an article in the *Harvard Business Review* where she claimed these leaders were wrong about the source of the disruption.

> *"My research and analysis reveals flaws in that thinking. It is customers who are driving the disruption. Disruption is a customer-driven phenomenon,"* she wrote.

Customer demands are changing faster than ever. The shelf life of solutions is getting shorter and shorter. Creating a culture of agility is more important than ever, and managing that culture remotely is quickly becoming a required skillset for all leaders.

We work with leaders across many industries as diverse as pharmaceuticals, retail, manufacturing, hospitals, and restaurants. All are feeling the pain of trying to get their teams to think differently. Think back to the 10–80–10 principle we mentioned in the Introduction. How valuable is that top 10% when it comes to moving fast?! Agility requires that employees refuse to deny the world has changed—permanently—and it demands letting go of the way we've always done things. The leaders who are able to get their teams to think and act differently are gaining market share. They are the ones being elevated in organizations and industries fastest.

HOW TO LEAD THE CHANGE

New ideas are critical, but coming up with them is not enough. Execution and implementation are just as important.

Here are four questions that will help you and your team be more agile. We've facilitated countless meetings with teams around these four questions and seen breakthroughs in their performance and culture. Virtual breakouts are the perfect tool to utilize this framework.

Question 1 (SEE REALITY):

What's the reality we most need to acknowledge?

- What changes have happened that we need to acknowledge (internally and externally)?
- How have the resources available to us changed?

Put it all out there when answering this question! Don't think about solutions yet—just list out what reality looks like right now.

Question 2 (TAKE OWNERSHIP):

How are we contributing to the problem and solution?

- What are we doing that's making our reality worse?
- What role have we been playing and what do we need to own?
- Where do we need to see greater involvement from this team?

Don't go to solution here—just talk candidly about your team's role in the situation you find yourself in.

Question 3 (CREATE SOLUTIONS):

What else can we do?

- Now that we've acknowledged reality and we know our role in it, ask: What else can we do to help deliver our Key Results?
- What have we not considered that we should be trying?
- What is working that we could lean into even more?

Brainstorm here! Get as many ideas listed out as fast as possible. Tap into the creative energy of your team.

Question 4 (EXECUTE NOW):

Who will do what, by when?

- Based on this conversation, what will each of us do individually in the next 30 days to help us deliver our Key Results?
- What are two or three things you will do, and by when?
- You may need to assign specific tasks to specific people; do so, and clarify the 'by when'.

Help your team be very specific here! Things like "collaborate more" or "reach out to more potential clients" aren't what you're looking for.

These are four powerful questions for individuals and teams to think through. They could be the agenda for a virtual meeting you lead. You could spend 10-15 minutes having your team discuss each question. You might want to divide the team up into small groups and have each team discuss the same question in a breakout room for few minutes. They could then come back and report on what they talked about. Do that for each question, and end the meeting with each person reporting on what they came up with for Question 4.

We've seen that process lead to breakthroughs in how a team thinks and acts. That's what managing culture looks like. No one knows everything that needs to be known about leading culture in a remote world. Agile leaders will learn the best practices and figure out how to get it right. They will be the disruptors.

Have you ever thought about what the market looks like for a leader known for their ability to get teams to adapt, shift, think differently, and deliver results?

It's enormous!

NEXT STEPS

▶ On your own, think through and answer the four questions posed in this chapter.

▶ Facilitate a discussion with your team around the four questions. Follow up a few weeks later to see who did what and what impact it's having on results.

- -

Tactic 8

DEMONSTRATE EMPATHY

---

12 TACTICS

1. CREATE CLARITY
2. GENERATE ALIGNMENT
3. BUILD ACCOUNTABILITY
4. BE VISIBLE
5. BE ACCESSIBLE
6. BE TRANSPARENT
7. INCREASE AGILITY
8. **DEMONSTRATE EMPATHY**
9. MANAGE BELIEFS
10. RUN EFFECTIVE MEETINGS
11. VALIDATE AUTHENTICITY
12. ENSURE WELL-BEING

W hen James Reed got the phone call, he quickly realized there was no playbook for any of this. While many industries suffered severe reductions in demand when Covid-19 hit, that wasn't the case for the trucking industry. Their workload surged. James is CEO of USA Truck, with offices right at the halfway point of the southern transportation corridor and not too far from the global headquarters of a little company called Walmart.

It was "all hands on deck" in the weeks after Covid hit for James, his leadership team, and their army of employees. As they struggled to keep up with demand, James got a call from a female employee. She reported that she might have been exposed to the virus. A family member had tested positive. Keep in mind this was in the early days of the pandemic, when we all knew so little about the illness and doctors were trying to figure out how to treat it. The employee hadn't tested positive, but she might have contracted it. James had to make a decision. He knew they had semi-trucks full of cargo that needed to be moved. And yet, as he told us the story in real-time, his mind wasn't as much on the product as it was on his employee.

"These are truck drivers," James said. "They get paid by the mile to move freight. In the course of speaking with her, I said, 'Just make sure you keep your healthcare paid and going so you can be treated for this. When you get back to work, we'll figure it all out.' She kind of laughed and said, 'I live paycheck to paycheck, and I pay for my healthcare out of those paychecks. What are you going to do for me?'"

"What I said to her was, 'Look, you know with your first kid you're the worst parent. You're experimenting on them.' I said, 'You're our first Covid-19 case. It's a great question you're asking, and we haven't really thought through it.' I was just trying to be transparent and honest and humble. I said, 'I don't know the answer, but I'll figure it out with you.'"

Who wants to work for a leader like that? What kind of culture do you think he's creating? James didn't delegate that conversation. He made the phone call and as CEO demonstrated what we're calling Tactic 8: Empathy.

WHAT IS EMPATHY?

Of all of the tactics that make up Remoteability, some might be surprised to see us include empathy. Don't be.

Conservative estimates show that depression symptoms have risen more than three-fold during the Covid-19 pandemic. It's a hidden side effect that might be worse than the actual pandemic. The data suggests that the need to "feel" with people, *your people*, your customers, has never been greater.

Even in the absence of a pandemic, it takes additional effort by a leader to make sure their remote team feels connected to the leader, each other, other departments, and the customer.

That feeling of connectedness starts when a leader intentionally demonstrates empathy. Let's get aligned around a shared definition of the word.

 Empathy: the capacity to understand what someone else is experiencing, from their frame of reference.

Empathy says, "I'll be present with you during your difficulty." It signals a willingness by a leader to jump in the trenches. Empathy isn't sympathy. Sympathy creates separation. Sympathy signals, "I feel bad for you, but I need to go back to work now." Empathy builds relationships. A leader who chooses to feel and express empathy is a leader focused on making connections. And in a suddenly remote world, more connection is exactly what is needed.

EMPATHY FOR THE CUSTOMER

"Steve Jobs was famous for never commissioning market research," James Allworth wrote in *Harvard Business Review*. Allworth calls empathy the most important thing he learned at Harvard Business School. Many have described the brilliance of Steve Jobs as being rooted in his habit of walking around the world and watching what people did. He'd then place himself in the shoes of his customers and relentlessly innovate around that need.

Spend some time studying companies that have been disrupted right out of their market and time and again you'll find companies that failed to look at the world through the lens of their customer. You don't need us to list those brands. You know them—companies blindsided by competition that had developed a deeper interest and concern for what the customer needed or wanted. It's what disruptive companies do. They feel deep customer empathy.

We've worked for many years with truly empathetic leaders. You feel the customer presence everywhere within their teams. You feel the presence of the customer as much in the support functions as you do working with the sales and marketing teams.

We've been in meetings involving senior leaders at Amazon, where their first leadership principle of Customer Obsessed is referenced *maniacally* as the lens for decision-making. That Amazonian discipline flows from a commitment Jeff Bezos made many years ago to not spend any time studying the competition—an exercise he viewed as a waste of time. He once famously said, "The most important single thing is to focus obsessively on the customer. Our goal is to be earth's most customer-centric company." And they just might be. His mindset is rooted in empathy for the customer and the customer feels it.

 Having that kind of customer focus on your suddenly remote team is critical. But how do you create or maintain that proximity to the customer if your team is much more removed from them now?

We've seen leaders invite customers to make brief appearances in their virtual meetings. We've also witnessed leaders who don't typically have a lot of direct interaction with the customer develop the habit of making one or two phone calls a week to customers. They rave to us about how it's helping them and their teams stay more connected to the customer, despite the new environment they find themselves in.

EMPATHY AND YOUR TEAM

So, let's get personal for a moment. How relatable or "real" are you? How approachable do people think you are? These are important questions, and yet we tend to judge ourselves based on our intentions rather than what we actually do. In other words, we might intend to be a caring, compassionate, servant-minded leader, and yet we don't always show up that way. Or maybe we rarely show up that way.

The irony is while we judge ourselves based on our intentions, we judge everyone else based on what we see them doing. We provide others with little benefit of the doubt. In other words, we lack empathy. Though the skill of empathy might not seem consistent with the modern concept of a traditional workplace—merciless, dog-eat-dog environments with employees reaching over each other to climb the highest peak—engagement of your team matters. And your team is obviously not living the same lives they were before the way we all work radically changed. Our point is empathy matters a whole lot more now than it used to. Skip this tactic and skill at your peril!

Now, we know we've been preaching in this little book about how nothing matters more than achieving the Key Results. That's #truth, but there's a reason we had to tell you about James Reed at USA Truck. You don't think every trucker in his company has heard that story about his call with that female employee worried about paying for her healthcare? What are the chances she got off her call with the CEO and didn't text or call any of her coworkers? We actually kind of like to visualize her walking over to a little wooden desk next to a stove fireplace, pushing the button on the CB radio and saying something like ... "Breaker, breaker, you got your ears on out there, boys? As you're looking out for the smokies on the interstate, I got some 4-1-1 for you. Boss man just told me he's gonna help me even though I might have the big Nineteen and be stuck in quarantine. You hear that? Someone over there at corporate's actually got a heart in their chest. Over and out, ya'll."

All right, maybe we watched way too much Smokey and the Bandit *when we were younger. For those of you under 30,* Smokey and the Bandit *isn't code name for something you buy with your med-card. It's a series we all watched before Marvel invented something called the action movie.*

Here's the point people... If your team feels like the only thing you care about are results, then kiss employee engagement and ownership goodbye. This isn't 1960 and you're not managing an assembly line. Results are what you're paid to deliver, but leaders who relentlessly focus on results at the expense of everything else can easily become a cancer on the culture. Isn't that an interesting paradox? Here you are taking a huge level of accountability for the results, and yet you might be responsible for turning the culture toxic! We've seen it happen. More than a couple of times.

 When members of your team log into a virtual meeting, they aren't transporting themselves into a different world. They're still parents, and now the kids are often on the other side of the wall.

Leaders who begin meetings and conduct business in a way that pretends life isn't challenging and changing in unique ways create a culture that lacks empathy and connection. That will impact results.

If you've ever worked with an extremely talented leader who also cared deeply about the input and abilities of others, you likely loved and thrived in that environment. It's an environment people connect with because it's an environment rooted in humanism and empathy. The loyalty and engagement created by empathy motivates team members to reach into the bucket of personal discretion and do a little more to deliver the needed results.

WAYS TO DEMONSTRATE EMPATHY

So, let's get more practical. What does empathy actually look like in a remote work environment? Here are several things we've seen leaders do that have demonstrated empathy and impacted the culture of their teams:

Allow a few minutes at the beginning of every virtual meeting for people to connect. This small talk used to happen in hallways as people walked to the meeting or in the room before the meeting officially started.

Log in to a meeting a couple of minutes early and take advantage of the opportunity to connect with members of your team. Ask questions and demonstrate curiosity about their lives.

Make a point of validating people's desire to turn their camera off temporarily as they grab a quick lunch during the meeting or deal with a disruption at home.

Allow people to call in to meetings when they're on the move. Make it acceptable behavior to dial in sometimes while picking up a child from school or heading home from a midday workout at the gym.

End meetings early when possible. Many times people have back-to-back virtual meetings and need time to use the restroom, refill their drink, let their dog out, or get a moment of sunshine or fresh air outside. Don't think for a minute that a better meeting is a longer meeting.

These are just a few of the things we've seen leaders do that make their remote team feel more connected and them come across more empathetic.

NEXT STEPS

▶ Try one of the tactics listed above to demonstrate empathy for your team.

▶ Connect in new and frequent ways with the customer so you can feel more empathy for them and serve them better.

MANAGE BELIEFS

---

12 TACTICS

1. CREATE CLARITY
2. GENERATE ALIGNMENT
3. BUILD ACCOUNTABILITY
4. BE VISIBLE
5. BE ACCESSIBLE
6. BE TRANSPARENT
7. INCREASE AGILITY
8. DEMONSTRATE EMPATHY
9. **MANAGE BELIEFS**
10. RUN EFFECTIVE MEETINGS
11. VALIDATE AUTHENTICITY
12. ENSURE WELL-BEING

hree deaths in one year. Each of the victims was under 30 years of age. All of them would have survived if they had worn their safety harness.

It was shortly after the third death that Jared found himself sitting in the office of the CEO. This leader was anxious to describe his company's commitment to safety. He rattled off a bunch of policies and procedures that should have prevented the accidents. He talked about the safety training meetings that were held regularly. This utility company prided itself on its commitment to safety, and this seasoned executive was laying out the evidence.

As Jared and our team dug deeper into that company's culture in the weeks after that meeting, we discovered something. The oldest and most experienced employees seemed to disregard the safety policies. They were the worst offenders when it came to not wearing protective gear. Yes, they had attended all the training meetings and knew the policies, but they disregarded them. Why? Well, because they had been doing this job for years and knew how to avoid the dangers of working on utility lines. They weren't wrong. The data did show the experienced employees weren't the ones who had been involved in any of the accidents.

What our team discovered, though, was the veterans were the problem. Here's why. Guess who the younger and less experienced employees were watching? Right! They were taking cues from the older teammates who went to the safety training meetings but disregarded the instructions. The newer crew members held a belief. They believed that safety harnesses weren't actually needed and that all the policies and procedures were a waste. Not only that, but they believed that the more seasoned technicians looked down on them for following all the rules.

THEIR BELIEFS SHIFTED

Jared pulled some of the older techs together and told them "you're killing these kids." They were shocked. They hadn't considered the impact of their unwillingness to wear the harness. One of the techs actually teared up. Jared asked them what beliefs they wanted the new team members to hold about safety and what experiences they were willing to create to ensure no one was ever hurt on the job. In that moment, the mindset of the more experienced team members shifted. They realized they were part of the problem. The change in the culture was palpable. Every crew member started wearing the harness every time. No exceptions! Many of them weren't wearing it because they thought they needed it but because they wanted the newer team members to be protected.

That change was captured in a statement we call a Culture Belief or Culture Behavior. We'll explain the process leaders can follow to come up with these statements in a moment. One of the Culture Beliefs that utility company adopted that year was:

Protect Everyone: I keep myself and others safe by doing EVERYTHING to ensure we all go home the same way we came in.

Over the next two years, the same team saw a dramatic drop in safety incidents. Not because they created new action plans, policies, or procedures. The improvement came because they addressed how the team was thinking. When you address mindsets that are creating barriers to your desired outcomes, you address behavior at the root cause. People self-direct the actions they need to take when their mindset is right. With the massive change to the work environment, to what customer interactions now look like, and to what it takes to deliver results, we are certain each of you reading this book needs shifts in the mindset of your team right now. You need them to think and act differently to help achieve the Key Results.

THE MINDSET NEEDED ON YOUR TEAM

Managing mindsets always starts with getting clear on the results your team or organization has to deliver. We covered that with Tactic #1. Once you know the three or four results your team has to deliver, the next question to ask is: "How are we thinking and acting in ways that are getting in the way of delivering our Key Results?" We encourage you to facilitate discussion around that question in one of your meetings. Allow time for a robust conversation. Encourage people to be open and honest. You might open a spreadsheet and share your screen to capture what the team offers in real-time.

> The two mindset questions to ask are:
>
> 1. How are we thinking and acting today in ways that are getting in the way of delivering our Key Results?
>
> 2. How do we need to think and act to deliver the Key Results?

Your spreadsheet should have two columns and look something like this:

	Current State	Future State
1	We don't take risks, too conservative, we suffer from analysis paralysis	We need progress over perfection, good enough will work
2	We don't speak up, fear of saying what we think	Open and candid communication is a must as it drives better results
3	....	....

After you build out this list, pick the top shifts that your team most needs to make in the next three to six months. Write a one-sentence definition that captures the essence of that mindset shift for your team. Finally, give it a two-word title that is action oriented—something like Own It, Take Risks, Speak Up, Work Together, or Focus and Prioritize.

Once you have clarity on one or two needed shifts, go to work on the new experiences needed to cement the new mindset. Everyone on the team needs to find ways to create experiences that will shift that belief. These experiences can happen virtually or in person. With a simple "constitution" to adhere to, these shifts become a clear lens through which a leader can evaluate, coach, and praise the team.

Understanding how your team thinks requires understanding two things: experiences and beliefs. People hold beliefs, and those beliefs are formed through specific experiences. To change a negative belief that currently blocks your path to Key Results, you need to strike at the cause of that belief. You need to replace the experiences that shaped those beliefs with ones that will inspire people to take the needed actions to get the result. Think back to the safety harness example and how the older technicians' experiences formed the younger techs' beliefs.

When poster campaigns are replaced by intentional experiences, created by a leader who is serious about leading change, a mindset shift becomes tactical and real. For example, when leaders intentionally focus in every staff meeting on recognition of the desired mindset, movement occurs. When they tell stories that illustrate what it looks like to demonstrate the desired mindset, movement occurs. When they seek and offer feedback focused through the lens of the desired mindset, movement occurs. Changing the mindset of the team or company accelerates when leaders evaluate performance, hiring, promotions, policies, procedures, and action plans through the lens of experiences and beliefs.

When it's all said and done, are you backing up what you're saying with what you're doing?

NEXT STEPS

▶ With your Key Results in mind, ask your team which shifts are needed in the way the team thinks and acts?

▶ Identify the 2–3 most important mindset shifts and craft a simple title and statement for each one.

▶ Begin creating new experiences around that shift. Model the mindset needed on your team.

RUN EFFECTIVE MEETINGS

- -

12 TACTICS

1. CREATE CLARITY
2. GENERATE ALIGNMENT
3. BUILD ACCOUNTABILITY
4. BE VISIBLE
5. BE ACCESSIBLE
6. BE TRANSPARENT
7. INCREASE AGILITY
8. DEMONSTRATE EMPATHY
9. MANAGE BELIEFS
10. RUN EFFECTIVE MEETINGS
11. VALIDATE AUTHENTICITY
12. ENSURE WELL-BEING

At the beginning of 2020, no one could have predicted that your new co-workers would include your cat, dog, parrakeet, and a cute six-year-old who seems to always want his grilled cheese in the middle of every staff meeting.

You've likely had enough experience with virtual meetings now to have participated in the good, the bad, and the ugly. You've discovered some of your co-workers are actually less tech savvy then your 89-year-old grandma. Find the mute button, Bernie!

 In many ways, meetings on Zoom, Teams, or WebEx can be much more efficient and effective than meetings in person. Yet, few of the leaders we work with seem to have developed an intentional virtual meeting strategy.

As we mentioned in the Introduction, we transitioned to almost all virtual meetings with our consulting clients after offices sent everyone home in early 2020. The transition for us was... well, let's just say we freaked out. Our hallmark for decades has been our ability to facilitate meetings that engage teams, move fast, and bring value.

We leveraged being in person to build meaningful relationships, read the room, and make needed adjustments to the agenda on the fly. We developed a reputation for meetings that generated movement in the culture and created alignment around the Key Results. Our clients often remarked that we had some kind of "secret sauce" in the way we facilitated meetings. Part of that "sauce" was creating an environment that required engagement.

We insisted on no tables in our meeting rooms. Just chairs, flip charts, and a screen. Within the first few minutes of every meeting—whether it involved thousands of people or a dozen senior executives—we broke the group into smaller work teams. You can hide in a meeting of a dozen people or more, but it's impossible to hide in a group of two or three.

When workforces transitioned to being remote, and after we finished freaking out, we went to work innovating. We had to find a way to replicate our in-person "secret sauce" in the new virtual environment. We're thrilled to say our clients believe we've done it. Before you skip the rest of this chapter thinking we're wasting your time patting ourselves on the back, we're giving you the background to help make the point that virtual meetings can be remarkably productive and effective in driving greater engagement, alignment, accountability, and collaboration. The same principles that create effective in-person meetings apply virtually. There's no need for a new set of rules.

THE TEN BEST PRACTICES

Here are the nine best practices our clients have shared with us for effective virtual meetings:

(1) **Start Casual:** Spend a few minutes at the beginning of a meeting catching up. Talk about the little things that you would normally talk about over a bagel in the back of the room before the meeting officially starts. These seemingly small things are what build relationships amongst team members and, when going virtual, the space for these small moments is harder to find. We work with the CHRO of a major healthcare system who will ask all of the pet owners on the team to take 30 seconds to share their most recent picture of Fido. Somehow, she remembers the names of most of the pets and follows up in future meetings on their welfare. Be deliberate about making time for relationship building in virtual meetings.

(2) **Focus on Results:** The best meetings have a clear purpose. Why are you having the meeting? Start your meeting by describing the purpose of the meeting and linking the output of the meeting to a specific business outcome such as profit, revenue growth, safety, customer satisfaction, etc. Throughout the meeting, revisit the business outcomes, connecting the meeting content to why you're spending time together. This simple habit will increase the value of your time together.

3 **Collect Data and Insights:** The tools built into most virtual platforms allow leaders to collect data and insights more efficiently than in any in-person meeting. The chat function allows you to collect perspectives from every single person, in matter of a seconds. In the virtual world, individuals who rarely speak up in group settings now have an equal voice. The polling function, as another example, allows you to pull in measurable data on important topics with very little effort. Data is a leader's best friend! Use these tools to gain a more accurate understanding of what's going on.

4 **All In or All Out:** Don't try to mix in-person with virtual. Go all virtual with each person at a computer or all live in the same room. It's hard to leverage the available benefits to either approach when you mix the participant experience. If you commit to one versus the other, you can design the meeting to reach its full potential.

5 **Don't Go Too Long:** We've found that a four hour virtual meeting can be very effective, but that's the outer limit. We've also found that breaks need to occur about every 60–90 minutes. When you do break, specifically ask people to leave their desk, walk around, get a snack or drink, and even go outside.

6 **Turn on Video:** If you were holding the meeting in-person before, require videos to be on in the virtual space. This allows you to read the room and know if you need to adjust pace, content, or overall direction of the meeting. Ensure this expectation is set prior to the meeting or you'll have a few terrified team members who are suddenly living the nightmare of showing up to work with their pajamas on.

7. **Use of Chat:** Chat has been one of the pleasant surprises of going all virtual. Think of a normal meeting, even a small one with only seven people in it. Respect and good meeting etiquette require that only one person speaks at a time. By the third comment, others who had something to say often give up or don't want to stomp the point into the ground. With chat, however, we have access to the stream of consciousness in the meeting that was previously hidden. Strategic use of chat also allows you to instruct people to use the chat to answer questions, conveniently creating a record for review at a later time.

8. **Breakout Rooms:** Require participation by breaking the room into smaller teams. The video breakout room feature in Zoom is an essential element to running an effective virtual meeting. Other platforms are working to add this feature, but until they do, we highly recommend Zoom as your virtual meeting platform. No one has a better breakout room capability.

The report from each breakout room can be lengthy; however, the chat feature offers a neat solution. As one group reports on what their group discussed, ask the others to have a spokesperson add their key learning from their breakout into the chat window. This allows leaders to view the discussion in the chat and ask for a deeper discussion on topics of interest. Using the chat feature along with breakout rooms improves understanding and alignment from the entire team.

9　**Use Formal Discussion Slides:** Add slides in your meeting deck that call for a reaction to specific questions. Title the slide "Discussion Question" to be clear you are looking for a response. When the slide comes up, give everyone time to process the question before asking for a response. This means you need to fill that space in time with something. With the question in front of the team, it's a great time to offer up additional data, personal insights, or a story that adds color to the topic. Then ask the question again, and add one more thing to ensure everyone has had time to process the question. Now ask for comments from the team. If you're getting crickets, put them into breakout rooms to discuss, or use chat to start the conversation.

10　**Change It Up:** Use a real flipchart or whiteboard to mix it up and engage the team. Many of us have set up a flipchart in the corner of our home office with a second webcam on a tripod to enable a quick change of scene. Just the other day we had a leader say, "Oh, a flipchart! It feels like it's been years since I've seen one of those." The use of different media can make a big difference in engagement with your meetings. Logging into the same meeting twice, with a tablet or iPad, allows you to share your screen on the secondary device while keeping your camera on. These devices allow tools such as digital pencils to draw or write where everyone can see the output. The key to this best practice is to keep moving and don't become stale.

We've been pleasantly surprised to find virtual meetings working just as well as what was previously thought to work only with face-to-face, in-person meetings. As you work to integrate the virtual best practices described in this tactic, you will see improved outcomes across your meetings.

NEXT STEPS

- ▶ Look at your calendar and identify one meeting that needs improvement. What best practices do you need to incorporate?

- ▶ After the meeting, ask your team for feedback on what worked and what can be better. Apply that feedback to next meeting.

VALIDATE AUTHENTICITY

- -

12 TACTICS

1. CREATE CLARITY
2. GENERATE ALIGNMENT
3. BUILD ACCOUNTABILITY
4. BE VISIBLE
5. BE ACCESSIBLE
6. BE TRANSPARENT
7. INCREASE AGILITY
8. DEMONSTRATE EMPATHY
9. MANAGE BELIEFS
10. RUN EFFECTIVE MEETINGS
11. VALIDATE AUTHENTICITY
12. ENSURE WELL-BEING

Do you remember the first time you turned on a webcam in your house during a work meeting? How much time did you spend cleaning up the room, angling the camera away from the furniture you've been meaning to replace, or figuring out where to put the dog? How concerned were you about your child's tantrum making its way into your team meeting? The massive and sudden shift to working from home left most leaders scrambling to find a spot they could go "live" from in the virtual space.

We'll never forget the first virtual meeting we facilitated with a client where one of the leaders in the meeting was holding a baby in his lap in his makeshift home office. What would have traumatized most of us, due to fear of looking unprofessional, is now accepted and even considered endearing behavior for most in virtual meetings.

The president of a global pharmaceutical company was recently expressing to us the gratitude he felt for having met most of his direct reports' children. He mentioned how that never would have happened in the world we used to know. He was genuinely excited about it and has encouraged leaders to not stress about trying to keep their family, or cats for that matter, out of view.

 The line between our personal and professional lives has never been thinner. The pandemic seems to have permanently dented the wall that used to exist between who we are at home and who we are at work.

We hope we never go back to having to pretend we always wear business attire and have spotless homes, silent animals, and perfectly behaved children.

Why does any of this matter? Or why should it matter to leaders who get paid to deliver results? The more authentic your employees can be at work the more engaged they will be in the work you need them to produce. It's not theory. It's what the data shows. Google "authentic leadership and employee engagement," and you'll encounter enough studies to keep you busy reading for the next several weeks. Surveys and studies show the more authenticity leaders demonstrate and the more authentic team members feel they can be at work the higher the levels of engagement and trust.

Deborah Woollard, a VP of HR at Cisco, said, "A lot of the persona you create when you go to work and keeping parts of your life separate—when you are working in a remote environment, a lot of that is being broken down. And I think one of the great things about the current situation is that rather than trying to hide it, it gives our employees the opportunity to say: 'This is me. This is my life.'" She made the comment to a media organization called People Matters, no less.

How do we as leaders create a culture that encourages and promotes authenticity in this new environment? Here are a few simple best practices we've seen.

1. VALIDATE AUTHENTICITY

This is as simple as giving people permission to have a messy background, a noisy environment, or minor disruptions during your meetings. Obviously, you want members of your team to focus, but in our experience most employees lean toward fear of being authentic rather than unprofessional or constantly distracted behavior.

We recently had an experience where one of us was racing home after working out at the gym. We didn't have time to change out of our workout clothes before a virtual meeting with a client. The meeting was a brief check-in with three HR leaders on a culture management project we're a year into. When we turned on our camera and they saw us looking more casual than normal, the Chief Human Resource Officer said, "I'm so glad you feel comfortable enough with us to come dressed so casual today." That comment validated authenticity. It allowed us to be our true self in that quick meeting.

Encourage people to turn their cameras on and not worry about what's happening in the background or how polished they look at the moment. Those simple words validate and provide cover for authenticity.

2. DEMONSTRATE AUTHENTICITY

A leader who logs into every meeting looking perfect or never being disrupted will struggle to create an authentic culture amongst their remote workforce. We encourage you to intentionally be more casual at times, or to start a meeting introducing your spouse or child in the background. Take your laptop and log into a meeting from the back porch or loft. Let down your guard a little, and let your team get a glimpse into your personal life occasionally. It's a new world, and small talk—where much of the relationship building occurs—is harder to come by. Demonstrating being human will build relationships and lower stress levels amongst the team.

3. HOST SOCIAL EVENTS VIRTUALLY

If you haven't been invited to a virtual happy hour, bingo night, or other online social activity, your time is coming. These events have an impact on a team's culture. They're as critical as in-person social events like holiday parties, awards banquets, and after-hours get-togethers. If you aren't the social type, then delegate the planning of one of these events to someone on your team who thrives on that stuff. We recommend doing something quarterly. It can be as simple as a 15-minute virtual huddle on a Friday where everyone wears jerseys from their favorite college team or as elaborate as a dress-up virtual evening awards banquet with produced videos and awards shipped out in advance. These events create unity and encourage authenticity.

NEXT STEPS

▶ Start your next meeting reminding everyone on the team that authenticity is not only allowed but encouraged during the meeting. Encourage them to turn cameras on and to not be concerned at all about messy rooms or noisy animals or humans.

▶ Intentionally demonstrate authenticity in an upcoming meeting.

▶ Schedule a virtual social team-building event in the next 90 days.

ENSURE WELL-BEING

- -

12 TACTICS

1. CREATE CLARITY
2. GENERATE ALIGNMENT
3. BUILD ACCOUNTABILITY
4. BE VISIBLE
5. BE ACCESSIBLE
6. BE TRANSPARENT
7. INCREASE AGILITY
8. DEMONSTRATE EMPATHY
9. MANAGE BELIEFS
10. RUN EFFECTIVE MEETINGS
11. VALIDATE AUTHENTICITY
12. ENSURE WELL-BEING

When Covid-19 hit, we'll be honest, we were kind of excited to take a break from airports and airplanes for a while. But then something weird happened. As the weeks of working in our home offices turned into months, we felt ourselves changing. Clothes that used to fit were now pretty snug (okay—they no longer fit at all). Walking up and down the stairs in our homes took our breath away. And someone was apparently breaking into our homes and stealing bags of potato chips.

Perhaps you gained the Covid-19 too. Not the virus. The 19 extra pounds. It turns out speed walking across parking garages, from meeting to meeting, through airports, to lunch appointments, and across the office building was actually pretty good for our health. Now our commutes were measured in steps, not miles.

Working remotely requires a more intentional focus on your health. Teams with leaders who look after their own well-being and are conscious about the well-being of their teams perform better. We're not just talking about physical health. This involves mental and emotional health too!

We mentioned the explosion in symptoms related to depression in Chapter 9.

 Research done by TotalJobs found working at home has led 58% of us to eat more than usual, 56% of us to be less active, and 45% of us to experience discomfort in our new workspace. Research published by Forbes showed 19% of those working from home report loneliness, 82% feel burned out, and 52% of us are working longer hours than we did when we went to an office.

Our own experience working from home, as well as listening to and observing our clients in hundreds of virtual meetings over the last year, gives us no reason to doubt these numbers.

PICKING UP PIGS

As long as we live, we won't forget a conversation we had with Tanner shortly after the Covid-19 pandemic forced everyone into this new dimension. It was apparent during a call we were on with him that he was driving on the freeway. As we were wrapping up the call and beginning our weekends, we asked where he was driving to. Tanner then provided this unforgettable response. "I'm headed to Nebraska with my daughter," he said. That response wasn't expected. So, we dug deeper. "Tanner, why are you going to Nebraska?" we probed. "If you really want to know, it's to buy some pigs," he surrendered.

"Pigs???" we shouted. Anyone who knows Tanner doesn't associate him with farm animals. He's more the Delta Sky Club kinda guy. After we stopped laughing, we had to know more. "My 16-year-old daughter promised when we moved from Georgia to Utah that she would raise pigs to raise money for her plans after high school," he said. It turns out Tanner was three years late on helping her make it happen. He had good intentions, but his travel schedule and other demands kept him from making good on his word. Covid-19 and this new work-from-home reality had removed every excuse.

TAKE CARE OF YOURSELF

The transition to remote work isn't all bad. There are some incredible benefits as well. Perhaps you're like us and have been spending more time with your kids, making time for hobbies you've always wanted to take on, eating lunch with your loved ones more often, going on more hikes, and pulling the board games out of the game closet. Maybe you too have said goodbye to good neighboring and started your own pig farm. With so much less time on the road, one of us coached a child's sports team for the first time in our lives.

This transition away from the office has allowed many of us to not only realize some changes in our lives were overdue but to actually make them.

While volumes of books have been dedicated to this particular subject, our only intent here is to provide you with a simple opportunity to evaluate your own well-being. As with all change, the potential for good and bad outcomes exists. Here are a few best practices for ensuring your well-being when working remotely:

Treat the start of the workday the same as when we had a commute to the office. Get up at the same time every day. Get dressed for work (even if that's more casual than before). Basically, develop a morning routine like you had when you went to the office.

Build in physical activity during the day and put it on your calendar. A bike ride with the kids after school for 30 minutes. An hour at the gym or a run outdoors. Lunch with your spouse or partner. Fifteen minutes to take the dog for a walk. If you don't put it on your calendar, you're likely to lose your day to appointments back to back to back.

Get out of the house at least once every day. Even a few minutes drinking a cup of coffee or hot chocolate on the back porch. A colleague of ours bought a simple golf net and hitting mat and spent 15 minutes a day in the backyard hitting golf balls. Even a quick run to a drive-thru does wonders for clearing your mind and keeping you fresh.

Set an end time every day. Lock in a time you leave the home office and log off. If you don't develop this habit, you'll look up from your computer and discover it's 9pm.

Schedule days off and unplug. Don't allow yourself to walk into your home office. You still need vacation days!

Keep unhealthy snack food away from your home office. Doritos and peanut M&Ms in your desk drawer is a disaster waiting to happen!

Allow yourself time on the phone with colleagues to just shoot the breeze. Some of us can get into the mode of trying to be too productive as leaders and not allow ourselves time to connect with the people we work with. Ten minutes of talking about your personal life with a colleague on the phone is an investment in your well-being.

TAKE CARE OF YOUR TEAM

Don't keep the things you're doing to ensure your physical, mental, and emotional well-being a secret. We encourage you, as the leader of the team, to intentionally share which of the above activities you did today or are making a habit of each week. When you do so, you give license to the members of your team to do the same. We have some clients that even start meetings occasionally with a "well-being minute," where someone shares something they did in the last 24 hours to stay mentally and physically healthy.

One long-time client, Brinker International—owners of Chili's and Maggiano's restaurant chains—has promoted the theme of #bestlife and encouraged team members at every level of the organization to tweet examples of getting into the outdoors, going on vacation, or having dinner at a fancy restaurant. The intent is to celebrate and promote well-being. Go to Twitter and search for "#bestlife" and "Chili's" to see the impact of promoting well-being so intentionally.

As a leader of a remote team, you can't just "keep an eye" on the well-being of your team. You have to specifically ask about it. Don't assume anything. Ask. That conversation can be guided by a few simple questions:

1. Before we talk about anything else, how are you doing, personally?
2. Are you finding the right balance between your work demands and your personal life?
3. How can I help you do it even better?

The healthier your team members are the more they're able to contribute to the Key Results. This point is related to what we discussed in Chapter 8 around empathy. An empathetic leader cares about the well-being of their team and demonstrates sincerity in their actions.

Harvard published research in 2020 that showed some good news about well-being when we shift to working from home.

Their research showed that, when shifting from working in a shared space to working remotely, the number of tasks we rate as tiresome drops from 27% to 12%. The study also found that when we work from home, we do 50% more activities through personal choice rather than because someone else asked us to do them.

It's incredibly important that we, and our team, are choosing to do "activities" that help us achieve our Key Results. But it's also important we're choosing activities that keep us healthy and performing at our highest level.

NEXT STEPS

▶ Do some of the things listed above to ensure your well-being.

▶ Share one of the things you're doing related to your well-being in your next team meeting. Make it a habit to allow some time for people to share what they're doing to stay healthy in your meetings from time to time.

CONCLUSION

- -

The future has changed directions. No one in today's workforce has experienced an event that more profoundly impacted the way people work than Covid-19. While no one can predict the future, we're confident the work environment has changed permanently. There's no going back to the way it used to be.

Covid-19 changed the way we interact with our colleagues and customers. It changed how we get things done. Among the thousands of leaders we, and our colleagues at our firm, interact with, not one believes the workplace of the future will look anything like it did before this massive shift to working remotely.

Leaders who demonstrate Remoteability will have the most opportunity *and* will make the biggest impact in the coming decade.

Yes, some of us will return to our offices. We'll once again see crowded factories or plants. Congestion on highways will get worse as more people begin to commute again. But how many days we spend in our offices at work each week, or how many meetings we fly people in to attend, or the percentage of people we hire who are required to live in certain cities or states will likely look very different than it did before this workplace revolution. A different way of working requires a different kind of leader.

We started this book with the 10-80-10 Principle, and we want to end it with that as well. Change is constant. Whether the change is brought on by a pandemic, competitor, or customers doesn't matter. What matters is how you as a leader react to those constant shifts. Do they paralyze you and send you into Panic Mode? Do they leave you awaiting direction as part of the majority of people in Stunned Mode? Or are you developing the capability as a leader to adapt quickly, create change, and help lead the way as one of the few energized by living in the Create Mode?

The 12 tactics we advocated for in this book will help you stake out your spot as a Creator, a Creator of a culture that produces results in this new work environment. You'll be a leader able to create clarity, generate alignment, build accountability, be visible, be accessible, be transparent, increase agility, demonstrate empathy, manage beliefs, run effective meetings, validate authenticity, and ensure well-being. The demand for that kind of leader is, and will be, significant.

Access the Online Tools

For help implementing these tactics and learning from others who are reading this book, log on to the free resources and course available at **remoteabilitybook.com.**

Train Leaders In Your Organization

For inquiries about purchasing this book in bulk for leaders in your organization, or for additional information about having us teach these tactics in a virtual workshop for leaders of your company, company, find out more by visiting **remoteabilitybook.com** *or send an email to* **info@remoteabilitybook.com.**

Made in the USA
Coppell, TX
11 March 2021